I0370688

Church Ethics
SPELLED OUT

Bobby L. Woods

Revised Edition

eta Publishing

Ocala, FL

Copyright © 2005, 2017 Bobby L. Woods

All rights reserved. No part of this publication may be reproduced, distributed, or transmitted in any form or by any means, including photocopying, recording, or other electronic or mechanical methods, without the prior written permission of the publisher, except in the case of brief quotations embodied in critical reviews and certain other noncommercial uses permitted by copyright law. For permission requests, write to the publisher, addressed "Attention: Permissions Coordinator," at the address below.

Zeta Publishing, Inc
3850 SE 58th Ave
Ocala, FL 34480
www.zetapublishing.com

The views expressed in this work are solely those of the author and do not necessarily reflect the views of the publisher, and the publisher hereby disclaims any responsibility for them.

Ordering Information:
Quantity sales. Special discounts are available on quantity purchases by corporations, associations, and others. For details, contact the publisher at the address above.
Orders by U.S. trade bookstores and wholesalers. Please contact Zeta Publishing: Tel: (352) 694-2553; Fax: (352) 694-1791 or visit www.zetapublishing.com

First published by Jean's Specialties in 2005

Rev. Date: 8/12/2017

ISBN: 978-1-947191-34-1 (sc)
ISBN: 978-1-947191-35-8 (e)

Library of Congress: 2017952544
Printed in the United States of America

There should be Order in God's House!
We Enter to Worship, We Depart to Serve.

Bobby *"Uncle Bob"* **Woods**
LOCAL SUNDAY SCHOOL SUPERINTENDENT, DISTRICT USHER PRESIDENT
STATE USHER PRESIDENT OF CENTRAL TN JURISDICTION C.O.G.I.C.

INTRODUCTION

THIS BOOK IS ABOUT CHURCH ETHICS

Not to be confused with biblical ethics which deals with rules for living righteously, doing what is good and refraining from what is evil.

Church Ethics deals with rules or guidelines for church behavior and mannerism.

The church is made up of many people with different cultural backgrounds, therefore, we must conform to similar guidelines for church behavior so that there might be unity in the physical church and that *"all things be done decently and in order."* [I Corinthians 14:40]

As we understand our place in the church and know how to behave ourselves as members of the body, we can serve in the ministry in a way that will bring glory to God.

Scripture references in this book are in italics and from the King James Version.

MY REASON FOR WRITING THIS BOOK

When I became a Christian, I lived in Dayton, Ohio. I joined a local church there and was trained to be a faithful devout Christian. After a few years of serving in the church, I moved back south to a small town in West Tennessee, where I grew up. I united with a local church in the small town of Bolivar. Immediately, I noticed things were done differently from what I had seen in Ohio. Some of the members did things without order or out of order. This was a wonderful group of people who loved the Lord with all their heart, loved each other, were Spirit filled, with superb hospitality, yet, sometimes they did things without order. As I visited other small rural churches, I noticed they too did things without order. This behavior bothered me. I was working with the Sunday School at this time. As I prayed concerning this matter, I heard in my spirit, "If the people knew better, they would do better." I went to my pastor and asked if we could include church ethics as a part of the Sunday School curriculum, and he gave consent.

This book is not about scripture or doctrine, even though I chose for a theme, I Timothy 3:15 which says, *"But if I tarry long, that thou mayest know how thou oughtest to behave thyself in the house of God, which is the church of the living God, the pillar and ground of the truth."* Paul writes to Timothy letting him know he wanted to come to him but was not sure when or if he would be able too. Whether he could be there or not, he wanted Timothy, the young pastor, to know how to behave/conduct himself in the house of God and to teach others as well.

I Corinthians 14:40 says, "Let all things be done decently and in order."

I thought I could just go to a bible book store and buy some literature on church ethics. I was surprised and disappointed because there was hardly anything on church ethics, nothing in detail or spelled out. So I began to teach church ethics, sharing what God was giving me.

I would be lying if I said everybody received it. Some rejected it; because I had no manual or literature to show. Some just didn't want to change; but, many received the teaching gladly and the church has been blessed.

Since our church is being blessed, I would like to share this information with others. This the reason for writing this book.

BECAUSE IT IS IN SIMPLE DETAILS, I CALL IT; **"CHURCH ETHICS SPELLED OUT"**

I pray it blesses you and your congregation!

CONTENT

SUBJECT	PAGE
Church Ethics	1
Do Only What is Asked Of You	
Devotion	
Scripture Reading	2
Prayer	4
Offertory Prayer	
General Prayer	
Benediction	
Facing Your Audience	5
Offering	
Announcements	7
Music During The Sermon	
Microphone Use	8
Walking During Worship	9
Talking During Worship	
Eating In The Sanctuary	
Chewing Gum	10
Choir Singers Manners	11
Handshaking	13
Holy Hug	14
Noise Pollution	15
Crying Babies	16
Dress Code	
Late Comers	18
Class Room Ethics	19
Respect The Teacher	21
Respect The Pastor	22
Respect For The Church	24
Communicate With The Pastor	25
Recognizing Visitors	26
Courting In Church	
Anointing Oil	27
Laying on Hands	

CONTENT CONTINUED...

SUBJECT	PAGE
Customs & Traditions	28
Decorations & Memorials	29
Credential Holders	
Pulpit Ethics	30
Ushers	31
Throwing Off	33
Proper Rebuke	
Understanding Rebuke	34
Overly Emotional	35
Drinks In The Pulpit	
Pulpit Aide	38
Coat-Tail Pulling Rule	
Associate Ministers	39

THOUGHT PROVOKING TOPICS:

Car Wash	40
Preaching Behind The Preacher	
Female Pastors	41
Pregnant Single Women	
Comments About This Book	42-45

CHURCH ETHICS
[spelled out]

As we strive for excellence, we will do better and become better if we keep in mind what Paul says to Timothy in I Timothy 3:15, "*I want you* to know how you ought to behave yourself in the house of God, which is the church of the living God, the pillar and ground of the truth."

DO ONLY WHAT IS ASKED OF YOU
When you are asked to do something in the church during worship, just do what you are asked. Should you find it necessary to do or say more; you should ask for permission. That's just good manners! Remember church time is prime time; don't waste it.

If you are asked to sing a solo just sing. If you must have words before you sing, as many do, (for whatever reason), let your words be short. You were asked to sing. The time you spend talking should be subtracted from your singing time. Don't make people glad to see you get up, and glad to have you shut up.

DEVOTION
Devotion, the beginning of the worship service, is an important and sacred time. It brings or ushers in the Spirit of Worship. Therefore, anyone conducting the devotional service should be Spirit filled, people who recognize and follow the leading of the Spirit. It is unethical to allow UNSAVED PERSONS to lead this service, especially when you know they are not Spirit filled or [Christian], of course, we don't always know.

From time to time I see children serving in this area. If you ask them are you saved? Their answer is "No". Do you want to be saved? Their answer is "No". If you ask the adult, why use them in this area? They will say, "We are training them up in the way they should go." I know what the bible says in Proverbs 22:6, but the devotional service is no time to play church or practice. I feel this type of behavior is actually training our children to be hypocrites. I don't think this is what the bible is telling us. Think about it!

SCRIPTURE READING

If you are asked to read a scripture during worship, you should give the chapter and verse(s) of the scripture you will read. Some people like to read along with the reader which is good. *You might be surprised to know how many people leave words out or add words when reading scripture.* Words such as; and, the, or, not, but and such like can change the whole meaning of the verse.

Always read loudly and clearly. Speak into the microphone. Always stop at periods and pause at commas, in other words, recognize all punctuation. Also, since the ***King James Version*** of the bible is standard among Christians, you should make it known before you start reading if you are reading any other version, that's just good church ethics.

You should not attempt to interpret the scripture; just read what is written with enthusiasm and clarity. Repeating words or phrases of the scripture reading should not be done because those who are not reading along with you, or those who are not familiar with the passage you are reading, will not know that it is not recorded as you have read.

Sometimes, it will be necessary or good to choose scripture that pertains to the occasion. II Timothy 3:16 reads, *"All scripture is given by inspiration of God and is profitable for doctrine, reproof, correction, for instruction in righteousness."*

All scripture is good, but all scripture is not appropriate for all occasions. If you ask a child or a new Christian to read, you should help them choose a scripture. I'll tell you why. A few years ago someone asked a new Christian to read a scripture. He commenced reading from ***Songs Of Solomon 4:1-5*** which says; vs. 1 *Behold thou art fair my love thou art fair; thou hast doves eyes within thy locks thy hair is as a flock of goats, that appear from mount Gil-e-ad.* vs. 2a *Thy teeth are like a flock of sheep that are even shorn.* vs. 3a *Thy lips are like a thread of scarlet,.* vs.4a *Thy neck is like the tower of David builded for an armoury.* vs. 5 *Thy two breasts are like two young roes that are twins which feed among the lilies"*. You must agree this is not the best choice of scripture for devotional reading. but a child or a new Christian does not know.

3

PRAYER

When asked to pray for or concerning something in particular, your prayer should be centered around that particular thing: For instance, *if you are asked to pray for the sick your prayer should be for the sick.* At this time, you would not pray for the mayor of your city and the president of the U.S., unless they are sick. These people need our prayers, but at this time just follow instructions, pray for the sick.

OFFERTORY PRAYER

During worship you are asked to do the offertory prayer, whether before or after the offering is collected, your prayer should be concerning the offering or giving. I need not say, praises, thanksgiving and expressions of gratitude should be a part of every prayer.

GENERAL PRAYER

During the devotional part of the worship service you may be asked to pray, at this time you are at liberty to pray for anybody, anything, any situation or whatever you desire. It is a general prayer.

BENEDICTION

At the end of service, if you are asked to do the benediction you may do it with a prayer, song or scripture. You may use your own words or any combination of the above, but it is not appropriate to do anything else. If you are asked to have words and dismiss, you are at liberty to have brief remarks. Remember when it's time to go home nobody, NO-BODY wants to hear anything you might have to say. So, practice good ethics, just do what you were asked to do.

If you are not the pastor, please do not ask; Is there any more business? Is there anything else to be addressed? If you ask and someone comes forward with something to be discussed, you automatically become the moderator of whatever business there is to be discussed. You have not been cleared to discuss any business. *You were just asked to dismiss.*

FACING YOUR AUDIENCE

When performing in church, you should always face your audience whether singing, speaking, teaching, or preaching. If you must turn, turn from side to side or turn your head. Never turn your back to your audience. Should you find it absolutely necessary to turn your back, you should make it as brief as possible, and turn again to face your audience. Turning your back to your audience is considered disrespectful and poor ethics. Stand erect. Don't lean or slump on the podium.

OFFERING

Offering time should be considered sacred, and it should be done in the spirit of worship. People participating in this part of the service should be trained, that things might be done in order. So often I see people just holding the tray as though they don't know why they are there.

When receiving an offering don't handle your own money. If you are collecting the offering you should put your offering in the tray before the collection begins or after it is finished. Don't put your hands in your pocket for anything after the collection begins; someone might think you are taking money from the offering tray. You don't want your good work to be evil spoken of. Don't allow givers to take their own change from the offering tray. That is your job. Be watchful of what goes in and give back the correct change. Never take your change out of the tray. [Example] If you are giving ten dollars out of a twenty, you should give it to someone else and let them give you a ten back.

Never allow yourself to be alone with the church money before it has been counted. Never give less than what you ask others to give. Ethics say you should give more than you ask of others. When handling church money, before it has been counted, there should always be at least two people. That way you might bear witness for each other.

When passing the tray come to the front of the pew so people can see you coming. They will get their money out and be ready to give. If you come to someone that is not making any effort to give just pass them by. Don't ever dangle the offering tray in a person's face. This is so embarrassing to someone who doesn't have anything to give. [*To the audience*] If you are asked to bring your offering to the table, everyone who is able to walk should walk even if you don't have an offering to give. It is better for you to walk so others on your pew will not have to climb over you going out and coming back in. Givers should not twist their money, make it into a ball or fold the money that you are giving. That is not good ethics. Some say it's an insult to God.

ANNOUNCEMENTS

Nothing should be read in the Church announcement concerning the church before it has been approved by the pastor or his designee. Time for announcements is basically for making known the final decision of any engagements/obligations which the congregation has.

Church announcements must be conclusive. There shouldn't be reason for questions or discussions; this can cause your announcement time to turn into a business meeting, which is so out of order. Apostle Paul said, *"Let every thing be done decently and in order"* [I Corinthians 14:40].

MUSIC DURING THE SERMON

Some ministers appreciate music being played while they are preaching. It has been said that music helps the preacher deliver his message. But if the message is delivered and cannot be heard because of loud music, the whole purpose is defeated. Therefore, if music is to be played during the sermon it should accompany and not dominate. The whole band or orchestra is not needed during the sermon. Drums, in my opinion, are not appropriate during the message. Thank you!

There is something else I see in some churches that bothers me. When musicians start playing all kinds of musical instruments very loudly just before the service begins or right after the benediction. Whether rehearsing or just messing around with the instruments, it is very disrespectful. During this time, worshipers old and young are trying to fellowship with one another and cannot hear themselves speak for the loud music. Some have not seen or spoken to one another for a week or more. This is the only time many Christian have for fellowship. Therefore, any music played during this time should be very soft. That's just good manners!

MICROPHONE USE

If you are singing or speaking and you are offered a microphone, do not refuse it. Even if you know your voice is loud enough to be heard all over the sanctuary; someone might be taping or listening from another room whereby your voice can only be carried by the P-A system. Many churches record their services now. If you refuse or leave the microphone your voice won't be heard clearly, and as a result you mess up the recording. So be sure you speak into the microphone at all times. If the microphone is stationary, don't walk away from it.

WALKING DURING WORSHIP

No one should be walking unless it be absolutely necessary during worship. The bible says, *"Keep your foot when you goest to the house of God."* [Ecclesiastes 5:1] If you need something ask the usher. The ushers will be glad to serve you. That is what they are there for. Please don't send a child, *when you send a child you are training that child to practice poor church ethic.* Some people will walk for any reason, it doesn't look good plus it can be very distracting. If you don't just have to walk, **Don't.**

TALKING DURING WORSHIP

Talking is a No, No! Not only is it bad manners, it could cause the person you are talking to miss their blessing. The devil takes every opportunity to work. It could be at the same time you are talking that something is being said the person you are talking to needs to hear. And because they are listening to you they miss their blessing. *No one should want to be guilty of that.* It's a distraction to the person you are talking to and to the person/persons that are performing and to anyone that can hear or see you. *It's just not good ethic to talk in church.*

EATING IN THE SANCTUARY

There should never be eating or drinking inside of the sanctuary. However, if a person is feeble because of age or illness and if it is inconvenient for them to go out to the water fountain and they are in need of a drink, the usher will serve them. But the church is no place for eating or drinking. Peppermints are no exception. I know we see it all the time, and we all have excuses for using it.

Some use it as a breath fresheners, but it's still candy and candy should not be eaten in the sanctuary during Worship. For whatever reason the candy mints are used, there must be substitutes. Some churches keep bowls of mint in the pulpit area and on the usher stand to serve special people during the worship services. *It may seem like a good thing, but it is poor church ethics.* No one should be munching on candy inside of the sanctuary during Worship.

I visited a church in Des Moines, Iowa where at some time during the service they take a few minutes break for fellowship. At this time, everyone is given a mint and a few minutes to meet, and to greet visitors and just fellowship with each other. I find this to be quite different from most churches. Yet in order, because they break from worship and go into fellowship. Otherwise, eating or drinking during worship is just plain bad manners.

Babies should not be given cookies, crackers, chips, candy, or any such things during worship. Babies may be given bottles but no food or candy.

CHEWING GUM IN CHURCH

Chewing gum in church is so ugly. Everybody knows it is forbidden, yet so many people still do it. When I put gum in my mouth, I used it as a breath freshener.

I always said, I won't chew it, I'll just hold it in my mouth, But I always found myself chewing it. Finally I stopped trying and found a substitute. It really looks bad when choir members are chewing in the choir stand or, anyone seated facing the audience. I've been told that gum should not be chewed in public and definitely not in church.

CHOIR SINGERS MANNERS

Many gospel singing groups that are considered professional singers have someone, usually the song leader, trained to excite the audience. They run or walk around in the church, up and down the aisles, sometimes jumping around, touching people, shaking hands as they sing and sometimes preaching trying to get people excited. They call this working the crowd. This kind of behavior might be okay for professional singers in an auditorium, but it is not appropriate or good ethics for a sanctuary choir during a worship service. Choir members should stay in their place, in the choir stand, sing to the glory of God and let the Spirit of God work the crowd.

Choir member should never be late. You should meet early enough to pray together before service begins; this is necessary. You are part of the ministry and your purpose is to help bring the audience into the spirit of worship. By praying together, you will be ready. All members of the choir should go to their seating area together and be prepared to stay. It does not look good when choir members are going in or out of the choir stand after service has started. *Please don't talk or chew gum, the audience is watching you.*

If choirs have been invited to take part in your worship, make sure the visiting choirs have time to share in the singing. It is not good manners to invite a choir and the home church choir sing several songs, use up all the time, and the visiting choir that came by request to render songs of praise, have no time or very little time to sing.

Choir members must be faithful for rehearsals. People can tell when you are lip syncing. If you don't know the song, you can't fake it. If you are with the choir when they practice a song they need you to be there when they sing the song. **Faithfulness is a virtue.** All choir members should do their best every time they are up singing, and sing as unto the Lord.

Some singers seem to hold back or not do their best for various reasons. For instance, if they don't like the song, if they can't lead the song or they have an ought against the song leader. Anyone with this attitude should not be allowed to serve in the choir. The first criteria for being a choir member is being a born again Christian and born-again Christians do not act like that.

If choir members are asked to wear robes or a particular color, please do what you are asked. Even if it's not your choice, uniformity is imperative! It makes a positive statement for your church. The way the choir looks and acts has a reflection on their pastor.

Some songs are actually a testimony. If you can't relate to the testimony, you should not sing that song. You can't give glory to God singing a testimony that is untrue to you. If you want the songs you sing to bless others, you need to sing songs with lyrics that bless you. Always sing songs that gives glory to God, please be mindful of that, because there are songs now that are labeled church/gospel songs, but they do not give praise or glory to God. *It is ethically incorrect to sing these songs during church worship.*

HANDSHAKING

Hand shaking is a part of fellowship. It is about physically touching a brother or sister. It is an important part of fellowship. So don't be offended when someone give a soft handshake, just remember what it is about, whether it is a firm handshake or a soft/flimsy handshake, it suggests, *I care about you and want to touch and feel your touch in the spirit of fellowship.*

Some people squeeze the other person's hand so hard until it's painful. If you have strong, powerful hands you can hurt a person with weak or delicate hands or people wearing rings. Keep these things in mind when fellow-shipping. Don't be upset if someone gives you their left hand, there might be a reason. Just remember what the handshake suggests, [*I care about you and want to touch in brotherly fellowship*]. Paul exalts the saints to; *"Salute each other with a holy kiss"* [Roman 16:16], this is making physical contact. Saints used to greet each other with a hug and a kiss, but

Satan found a way to steal both of these from us. He never misses an opportunity to work. He has stolen the hug and the kiss and now he is trying to steal the handshake.

HOLY HUG

Because of carnal thinking, many Christians feel that it is unethical for men and women to hug, but hugging or embracing is a part of fellowship. I've observed men and women trying to hug without their bodies touching as though they are afraid of each other. They lean in and reach out with their arms, turning their bodies in the opposite direction of each other allowing only one shoulder to touch. Remember, *we hold citizenship in two kingdoms: one is heavenly, the other is earthly.* In our heavenly kingdom, there is no sex. So, when we come together in worship and fellowship, let's operate in this heavenly privilege. Let's embrace each other.

Definition: HUG- *to embrace; to put one's arms around in greeting.* When two Christians fellowship in this manner with the right frame of mind and in the right spirit; God is pleased and he will work in the midst. The devil beats and pulls on the saints all week, but when they come together and embrace making physical contact, they transfer and impart strength one to the other. I have experienced it myself, and I've seen it time and time again. Christians receiving strength, being encouraged, healed and delivered though a simple *'Godly Hug'*. I want every Believer to realize, when we allowed Satan to steal the *'HUG'* we suffered a great loss. So let's hold on to the handshake, and work on taking back *our Godly Embracement, 'THE HUG'.*

NOISE POLLUTION

It is sad to say, but in many of our churches today we do have _noise pollution_. Older people are having to move from where they would desire to sit in the church to a less noisy area. Yes, I believe in praising God with a loud voice. The bible says make a joyful noise unto the Lord. Yes, I believe that we should lift up our voices like trumpets. Yes, I believe in loud singing, shouting, even screaming when the spirit of God gives utterance.

Again, the bible says, _"Make a joyful noise unto the Lord"_. The pollution is not in the voices it is in the musical instruments. Music should accompany voices and not dominate them. Organs and drums seem to be the major problem. I observed a drummer wearing ear plugs as he played his instruments. If the music is unbearable for the musicians, it seems they would know it is too for others! Sometimes, I think they are in competition for loudness. Every musician seems to be trying to play louder than the other. When someone is singing all music should be adjusted so that the voices can be clearly heard. The greatest problem with musical instruments is that they are just being played too loudly during worship service, even when the preacher/speaker is expounding God's Word.

P.A. (public announcement) systems also cause problems in many churches today. If the system is of poor quality you will never get a balanced sound; likewise, the speakers must be of high quality. When the speakers and the system are set right and operated correctly you should get basically the same sound throughout the sanctuary.

CRYING BABIES

If your baby starts crying in church and you cannot get it quieted, carry it out and take care of it. Don't wait to be asked. No one wants to ask a mother to take a child out of the church; but, you should not let them disrupt the services. Mothers you are not expected to run out of the church with your baby/ies every time they make a little noise. But, it is disruptive to just sit and let the baby continually cry and disturb other worshipers. Mothers be advised, don't trust your baby with just anybody even if they are wearing white. These are evil times. If your baby needs to be taken out during the service, carry it yourself.

I feel sorry for some minister's wives with small children. So often I see mothers trying to care for their children, sometimes two or three. And *the father does nothing, just sit in the pulpit like he doesn't know whose kids they are; running all over the church.* This should not be. It is both parent's responsibility to help keep order in God's House.

DRESS CODE

Some religious groups or sects such as Mormons, Mennites or Monks have special uniform or dress codes. But as Christians, we have no particular dress code; nevertheless, the bible gives us some guidelines such as; "Dress as becoming holiness" and "Adorn yourself with modest apparel." [I Timothy 2:9&10] Anybody in their right mind wants to look nice, and you should. When you go to the House of Worship you should be clean and dressed up. Be your best, and look your best. But remember; dress with modest apparel, not sexy, *you don't have to be a sex symbol to look good*, and you don't want to dress so fancy or flashy that you distract people from worship. [I Peter 3:3-4]

Women who are married to ministers should know that *the way you dress will have an effect on your husband's ministry.* Also, if their children's apparel is less than modest, that too, will have a negative effect on his ministry.

There are complaints concerning large hats. The problem being, when women wear very large hats in church the person seated behind them cannot see what is going on up front. Don't be a distraction to your fellow worshipers.

Ethically, what should be done if a minister is preaching and woman comes in off the street wearing a very short dress and sits on the front pew? This question was asked as I conducted a seminar on church ethics. Some suggested asking her to move back one pew; some said give her a cloth to cover herself. I suggested, you do nothing. You don't want to embarrass her by covering her. This is common dress for unsaved women, and if she doesn't have enough God to know how to dress she is sitting in the right place. The old folks called the front pew *the mourners bench and reserved it for sinners seeking salvation.* You shouldn't have to protect the preacher. The bible says a minister should wait on his ministry. If a preacher has not overcome lust, and needs to be protected from seeing a little skin ***maybe that brother should still be waiting, not preaching.***

Minsters and Deacons; Sometimes you will need to dress to look like the minister you claim to be. Wearing gym shoes, jogging pants, sweat suits, and shirt tail hanging out, can be a very comfortable way of dressing. But deacons and ministers; you are men in leadership. You might have to give up that comfortable way of dressing for church wear, because there are so many people who think ministers should be conservative in their dress and they can't receive you any other way, [*these people are called babes*]. In order to minister to these people, you might have to give up the comfortable leisure dress style. This comes under the heading of *longsuffering*. Sometimes, you just have to look the part.

LATER COMERS

Tardiness is extremely unethical. I cannot over emphasize how bad tardiness is. It is disrespectful to the house of God, the people of God and to God himself. This is crucial for people in leadership because some people will pattern after you. If your being late causes the service to begin or end later than the scheduled or expected time, some people will be angry and resent you. Some will actually leave the church and many visitors will not return. All of this is detrimental to church growth. It exemplifies a lack of discipline. As Christians, we are a people of discipline, and leaders must practice discipline. Every member of the church should be in the church ten to thirty minutes before the scheduled time of service. For instance, if service start at 10:00 A.M., all members should be in the building by 9:30 A.M. and no later than 9:50 A.M. Then you will have time for fellowship before worship begins. God wants us to have fellowship with one another. Many of us go to the same church and worship together for years and never get to know each other. We don't take time to fellowship. How can we share brotherly love to one another and meet the needs of each other? How can we know one another's needs when we don't know each other? So, don't be guilty of tardiness. Anyone who comes in after the service starts should be seated in the rear of the church.

The church is for fellowship and worship. Fellowship develops relationships with one another, and worship develops a relationship with God. Both are important for Christian growth and wellbeing. So, if you practice good ethics, be at church on time, then you will be blessed, and you will be a blessing to your fellow worshipers.

CLASS ROOM ETHICS

Teachers must be in the classroom and prepared to teach before students arrive. Students should not have to wait for the teacher. Teachers should never make excuses for not being prepared. In classroom discussions, new Christians will use themselves or their spouses to make a point or to make others understand their thoughts on the lesson; thereby, bringing their personal problems into the discussion. When this happens, the teacher must act with wisdom. Stop the discussion and refer that person to the pastor or to someone who can give them advice in a private setting. It is not proper to discuss any one's private life or situation in a classroom setting. In every discussion, there is a positive and a negative side. Both sides need to be heard to get a full understanding of what is being discussed.

In any bible study, a good teacher will relate the lesson to this time, this place and to the people they are teaching. They will relate it to the church community but to no church in particular. Never ever discuss the church you attend or any individual of your church. If you do, I will assure you somebody will be offended and rightly so. That's just not good ethics. If you are a bible teacher in your local church, use only literature published by your denomination or supplied by your local church. Any other literature should be inspected by the educational director or the pastor; because if everybody is allowed to use any literature they want, sooner or later somebody will be teaching from literature that is in conflict with your church doctrines.

If there is a question on the floor and you want to answer it, make sure you understand the question. Make your answer direct and to the point. Using the least amount of words possible. I've seen people take up to five or six minutes of prime class time answering a question. When they are finished; the person who asked the question gets up and says, that is not what I was asking. When

Church Ethics

asking a question, make your question as direct as possible and you might get a direct answer. In bible study, you should never argue your thought concerning the scripture whether you are right or wrong. You will never get everybody to agree with you. Arguing is so ugly; you can't prove yourself to be right by arguing. You'll only prove you are immature. If you are one that argues, I admonish you to *"Study to be quiet"* [I Thess. 4:11], in other words, 'Shut-up & Grow-up'.

RESPECT THE TEACHER

In the classroom, the teacher is in charge. It doesn't matter who else is in the class; the teacher should be respected as moderator. Many times, if there are bible scholars or anyone well versed in scripture, especially the pastors or elders, students will direct their questions to these persons, disregarding the teacher. That is disrespectful to the teacher who has prepared to teach this lesson and answer questions. *Such behavior is ethically incorrect.* All questions should be directed to the teacher who might give an answer or ask for comments from class members. However, if a student wants their question answered by someone specific in the class, they should acknowledge the teacher and ask to direct their question to that person. That's good ethic, that's respecting the teacher, the teacher deserves that respect.

I've been in class where people would interrupt the teacher with a question or a comment as soon as he/she gets started with their opening presentation. If you give the teacher time to make their presentation you will find, in most cases, many questions will be answered. Never interrupt the teacher even though some teachers talk too much. If you have a question or a comment, you should raise your hand or stand up and wait until the teacher recognizes you.

RESPECT THE PASTOR

Some people seem to think respecting the pastor means calling their name every time they are up to say or do something in the church. That is not respect necessarily, that is acknowledgement or recognition. In simple layman terms, *'respect the pastor'* means, *'obey', 'follow leadership' 'work with his program', 'do what you can to make his job easier'*, in other words; ***"Let him pastor you"***.

If you happen to be in a bible study with your church group and your pastor makes a mistake interpreting scripture, and he will, sooner or later, no one knows it all and very few, if any, get it right every time. So, if your pastor makes a mistake it would not look good for you to correct him openly. However, if the wrong interpretation of the scripture in question could be misleading to others and you have the answer or the correct interpretation you should bring it to his attention in private. He will appreciate it. If he is a big enough person to be a pastor, he will be big enough to go back and make the correction to the group. Don't go back and show the group where the pastor was wrong, but practice good church ethics, show the pastor his mistake and let him make the correction.

In every congregation, there will be people who will have more influence on some member of the church than the pastor. If you find that there are people in your church who looks to you for instructions and directions as though you are the pastor don't beat up on yourself. It doesn't mean you are doing something wrong. People are just that way. Nevertheless, once you realize this is happening it would be ethically incorrect for you to hold these people to yourself. You should point them to the pastor, and do all you can to build your confidence in the pastor as their leader.

If your pastor is asking you to do something that you feel is too much or you disagree with, remember, the pastor is human and a brother. You can talk to him. By communicating you could come to an agreement. If you cannot reach an agreement I suggest you try doing what the pastor asks. Sometimes, the pastor can see qualities in a person that they don't realize they have. It is unreal to think you will always be in agreement with everything the pastor does or says; but you should always speak words to build him up. If you talk negative about your pastor, you not only hurt him but yourself as well. Remember, *a people can be no greater than the pastor they follow, and by the same token, a pastor is no greater than the people he leads.* If you want a better pastor, speak more words about him that builds character.

When your pastor *or anyone* is preaching, everyone should be attentive. It is alright to read your bible along with the speaker, but when they close their bible you should close yours. It is very disrespectful to continue reading while the speaker is preaching. Church folks do many things out of order while the pastor is preaching. I've seen people writing checks, balancing check books, preparing offerings. All these things should be done before or after the sermon. I once saw a sister sitting on the front pew reading a newspaper as she listened to the Sunday morning sermon. This behavior is very disrespectful. Remember, we are to treat others as we wish to be treated, that means your pastor also.

RESPECT FOR THE CHURCH

If you use bibles or hymn books that belong to the church don't leave them lying on the pew. If you took it from the back of a pew, that is where you should put it at the end of the service. If you receive church programs or other literature, take it with you. Don't leave it on the seat or on the floor.

Put your gum in the trash before you enter the church. If you are inside the church and you realize you have gum in your mouth,

Church Ethics

wrap it in paper and put it in your purse or pocket… swallow it if you must. P-l-e-a-s-e don't leave it in the back of a pew and please, p-l-e-a-s-e don't stick it under the pew. Don't allow small children to have food, candy, or anything that might soil or damage seats and clothing.

Chewing gum should <u>not</u> be discarded on the parking lot. This causes problems when it gets attached to the sole of someone's shoe and tracked inside the lobby and sanctuary.

COMMUNICATE WITH THE PASTOR

Any pastor knows he can't pastor a church alone. It is just too much for one person; he has to have helpers. So the pastor looks in the congregation and finds people with leadership abilities and appoints them presidents or superintendents over various auxiliaries. Anyone holding this position is actually a supervisor; the pastor is head of all auxiliaries. So if the supervisors are to be successful, they must be in communication with the pastor. The supervisors need to know what the pastor wants them to do, and the pastor needs to know what the supervisors are doing. Don't ever take your pastor for granted. Before you start any program or set any idea in motion, make sure your pastor know exactly what your plans are. You might have a good plan or a good program, but it won't work for long without the pastor's endorsement. You might have a good idea, but if it doesn't work with the pastor's overall program it is no good. Therefore, communication is essential.

RECOGNIZING VISITORS

To most people it is an honor to have their name called in church, but to others it is offensive or embarrassing. There are people who won't go to church for fear of being made a spectacle. Some just don't want their names called, and they have that right. So, if a visitor does not fill out a visitor's card their name should not be called. Some people want to be seen and heard; others want to just blend into the crowd. The church does not want to embarrass anyone. Visitors should be given an opportunity to have words, if time permits, but never insist.

COURTING IN CHURCH

Occasionally, I see husband and wife sitting one in the others arm, not just an arm laying casually on the back of the pew but sitting pressed against each other as you would expect to see in a movie theater. It does not look proper because everybody does not know the couple is husband and wife. I realize courting is more than just sitting in one another's arms. What I call courting is; *when two people that are attracted to each other take the occasion to focus on one another, enjoying each other in a romantic way.*

Now, the husbands and wives that sit like this in church may not be courting. Maybe, they can sit that way and not be distracted. The problem is what we do, we give consent to. The youth will do what they see the adults do. It is happening! Saints are sitting in the front of the church embracing the gospel, and their children are sitting in the back embracing each other, "They are courting." If one adult couple sits in this manner at church during worship, it won't be long before young people will be doing it too. ***Imagine walking into the church and finding people all over the church sitting in each other's arms.***

ANOINTING OIL

It is not appropriate to use anointing oil on everybody who comes to the altar for prayer. The bible says, *"Is any sick among you? Let him call for elders of the church; and let them pray over him, anointing him with oil in the name of the Lord: and the prayer of faith shall save the sick, and the Lord shall raise him up..."* [James 5:14-15]. It speaks concerning prayer for the sick, but people come to the altar for many other reasons.

Oil should never be put on a person unless that person understands what is being put on them and why. Some people are not familiar with the practice of using oil and won't understand what you are doing. Some will think you are practicing voodoo, witchcraft, etc.

LAYING ON HANDS

Many people have been offended because of how and where they were touched while being prayed for at the altar. *"Brethren, I would not have you ignorant concerning these thing,"* the bible says, *"The prayer of faith shall save the sick."* [It is not your hand]. You don't have to touch where it hurts. Jesus touches people on the head and on the hand. If there are any doubts about where or how to touch a person while praying for them; *mark the perfect man,* JESUS.

RUBBING IS OUT! You never know who [or what] you are rubbing. We have now supposedly men trapped in women's bodies and women trapped in men's bodies. Some don't know what sex they are, so if you are rubbing someone's back or belly you might be doing more harm than good. *If you are trying to rub the pain out you need a liniment not holy oil.* (Bear with me in my humor).

CUSTOMS & TRADITIONS

When visiting other churches or worshiping with churches outside of your denomation, don't try and change their customs or traditions. You are the guest; don't insult your host, by holding onto your traditions. The bible says, *"When in Rome, do as the Romans."* For example, if in your church everybody stands for scripture reading, for you not to stand would be out of order. By the same token, if you are visiting a church that practices sitting during Scripture reading and you stand you are out of order. Follow the lead of your host whether you agree or disagree, **if it is not a sin.** That's proper ethics.

DECORATIONS & MEMORIALS

To decorate the inside of the sanctuary with pictures of people is not good ethics. Only pictures of Christ should be displayed inside of the sanctuary. Photographs of pastors, pastor's wives, pastor's children, former pastors, founding pastors or bishops, should be displayed in the vestibule, halls, memorial rooms or fellowship hall. ***Pioneers and noble people should be honored and remembered, but the sanctuary is not the proper place to hang their pictures.*** Many churches have scriptures displayed neatly in special areas of the sanctuary; this is in order. Pictures of people should not be displayed in the sanctuary, regardless of their greatness or legacy...

CREDENTIAL HOLDERS

It is not good ethics to put titles on our own name when speaking of yourself in general. In ministering to people you'll get better results by bringing yourself down to their level [sister/brother]. To refer to yourself as deacon, missionary, elder or bishops will be received as tough, you are exalting yourself above others. Paul said, *"I became as all men that I might save some."* (1 Cor 9:20-22). When introducing yourself you simply use your name. Example, my name is Praise Day, not Reverend Praise Day. If it is necessary for your audience to know your title as an office of the church, you simply state it. Say I am a deacon, an elder, a pastor or whatever the case may be. You should never say my name is Deacon, Elder or Reverend so and so. It makes people think you are anxious to let them know that you hold a position.

PULPIT ETHICS

Good ethics are crucial in the pulpit. Everyone else may do all they can to create a spiritual atmosphere in the church, but if people on the pulpit don't practice good church ethics, those in the audience will be turned off and possibly miss their blessing. When I say pulpit, I'm speaking of the platform that is usually raised higher than the regular floor so the speaker can see and be seen by everyone seated in the sanctuary. This platform was designed to seat those who were to appear on the program. Now it is used mostly for preachers as a way of showing honor or respect to those that preach the gospel.

When seated on the pulpit one should be mindful or careful of how they sit whether male or female. The way one sits can be embarrassing or even offensive. Once you are seated on the pulpit, you should be prepared to stay until the end of the service. If you know you will be leaving early, you should not take a seat on the pulpit.

Visiting ministers should never seat themselves on the pulpit without being invited. It is better to be asked up than to be asked down. People that are to be seated on the pulpit should be in the church and their place on time or at the beginning of the service. Should you come in late and you are not on program, don't expect to sit on the pulpit. It would be good manners to decline if invited by an usher because you will take the attention of all who are in attendance, but if you are invited openly by someone from the pulpit you should go because you have attention of everyone already; however, *you should go in shame for being late.* Remember all ministers or people holding leadership offices are automatically in the business of reproduction of character, and you can only reproduce what you are. *So if you are in leadership and you practice coming to church late you should always sit in the back of the church along with your production, those you have trained to be late comers.* The back seats are for late comers. If for some reason beyond your control you come in late and need to sit on the pulpit you should do it as unnoticeably as possible. Take the first seat available and sit immediately. *P-l-e-a-s-e do not go all over the pulpit shaking hands and fellowshipping with everybody that's seated on the pulpit.* **That just isn't good ethics!**

If you are given the opportunity to preach/speak and are given a time limit, you should do it within that time or less, **no exceptions.** I've heard people say, "They gave me fifteen minutes, but if the Spirit come in I may stay longer." **This is unethical and unacceptable.** The Spirit of God agrees with the word of God which says, **"Obey them that have rule over you."** Any spirit that tells you to do otherwise is the wrong spirit.

USHERS

The usher should never point anyone to the pulpit. Any person who is the be seated on the pulpit should be escorted by an usher. The usher should wait until the person has been seated or received by someone on the pulpit. It is important that an usher is seen escorting any minister to the pulpit after service has begun or people will think the minister just walked up on his own. The usher should never bring a minister to the pulpit to be seated without knowing for certain seats are available.

Remember ushers, being in uniform does not give you the right to walk or move around excessively. Ushers serving in the aisles can minimize walking by standing near the available seats and letting the guest come to you. It is not necessary to escort every person that comes in to be seated. If you stand near the available seat you can just point to the seat. Using the signal code minimizes walking. Any usher that does not know the usher's signals should not be allowed to serve. *"If an usher does not know the signals he/she just doesn't qualify."*

All ushers should be in full uniform when serving, uniformity makes a statement. When all are dressed alike it says, ***"We are ready", "We are together", "We are not individuals but one unit".*** To alter your uniform makes a negative statement. It makes the same statement our boys make when they wear their pants hanging off their behinds. It says, *"I'm rebelling against the system; I'm an individual; I'm my own man, nobody can tell me how to dress."*

THROWING OFF

If you are teaching, preaching, or making a speech from the pulpit, never take the occasion to say something negative to or about someone that is in the audience that you have an ought against. If you have a problem with an individual, you should tell them in private. To throw off is unethical and rude. It's just wrong! I've known ministers to use this method as a form of open rebuke. They bring up an accusation and say the person or persons I'm talking about or to, know who they are. They call it open rebuke, but it is not proper rebuke. I call it, *"dignified gossip."* The guilty party, if guilty, might know who they are, but others don't know who they are talking to or about. So they become suspicious of each other and start guessing and accusing one another. It actually brings division among the brethren. I know Jesus did something like that at the last supper but remember, *Jesus was prophesying not accusing the brethren.* It's Satan's job to accuse the saints.

PROPER REBUKE

The proper way to openly rebuke is to call the person out by name where there can be no misunderstanding as to who you are talking to. Present the accusations openly and give the accused person a chance to explain, deny or repent for the accusations. This way there is no room for misunderstanding or confusion.

People in leadership, especially Pastors, have to be strong but meek, gentle but firm, and above all they must be wise. They must also have a great love for people. Anybody possessing these qualities will not easily forget that *rebuke is to <u>help the person</u> that is being rebuked. It is not to be used as a way to get back at someone you are angry with, or to give someone a peace of your mind.* Rebuke is to help the person or persons who have done wrong get back on the right track. Once rebuke has been properly administered, you should move on. Whether it is received or rejected, you must forgive and move on. This issue shouldn't keep coming up every Sunday in the Sunday morning sermon. If the pastor doesn't forgive and move, rebellious people can and will cause him to become bitter. A pastor with a bitter attitude will bring much hurt to the body without realizing it.

UNDERSTANDING REBUKE

Not every person that messes up or makes a mistake in the church is worthy of rebuke. Any new Christian that is zealous is apt to make mistakes. If you beat them down by rebuking them every time they make a mistake, it won't be long before that person stops trying to do anything in church. Sometimes, a person just needs correction and training. Know, also, you don't rebuke people necessarily but spirits, such as; haughty, disobedient, or proud spirits within the person. Jesus rebuked Peter because of what he said, (Matthew 16:22-23) Paul rebuked Peter because of something he did, [*removed himself from eating with the Gentiles, Galatians 2:12*]. In the case with Jesus it was Peter's words; in the case with Paul it was Peter's actions that manifested or made known the spirit that had come on Peter. So Jesus and Paul were rebuking the spirits in Peter.

OVERLY EMOTIONAL

Ministers who cannot control their emotions while delivering sermons will hinder their own ministry. It doesn't matter how great the sermon is, if the speaker is moving or shouting excessively people will be turned off. Moving and shouting excessively causes some people to miss what is being said due to watching what is being done. A constant pace back and forth, while speaking, is so annoying to some people they actually close their eyes. So they can hear and receive what is being said and not be distracted by what is being done.

All ministers should seek training after accepting their calling. Some ministers think to be a good preacher or teacher, all you need to know is the bible, but if you don't know and practice good church ethics and control your emotions you will hinder your own ministry. You might feel like running, jumping and screaming, but if you over do it, it will take away from your ministry. Every minister is obligated to protect their ministry. I Corinthians 14:32 says, *"The spirits of the prophets are subject to the prophets."*

DRINKS IN THE PULPIT

Drinking in the pulpit is not good ethics, however, it has been widely accepted in the church community that we serve water to people who exert themselves during the services. To serve preachers or teachers during or after a sermon is a rule. When the usher serves these people, it should be water only, *except when the person being served requests something different or has a special need,* such as diabetics may need orange juice. Otherwise it should be water only, not a large glass, no more than six to eight ounces. You are not trying to fill bellies… you are only trying to refresh the person who has exerted themselves in the services.

Those who are served water while seated on the pulpit should drink it and return the glass to the usher as soon as possible, it is not good ethics to sit and sip during worship.

Ice cold water or water with ice cubes should not be served to anyone after exertion. The shock of drinking ice cold water could have severe negative effects. I witnessed a preacher, Elder Willie D. Mitchell, collapse and fell to the floor when he was served a glass of ice water after preaching.

I'm an usher; therefore, pastors and ministers tell me to stop the children from going to the water fountain saying, "They can survive for an hour or two without water." But fifteen minutes into the service, people on the pulpit are asking for water or juice. Is this ethical? I think not!

Years ago you could find only one or sometimes two preachers in the pulpit at the same time so then drinking didn't look so bad. But today you might find nine or ten preachers in the pulpit at the same time. Imagine the ugliness of ten people drinking and sipping water, all kinds of juices, teas and even soda pop during worship service. *You have never seen ugliness until you see ugliness in the pulpit.*

Bishop L.H. Ford who was the Presiding Bishop of the C.O.G.I.C. at the time, made a statement during the Convocation in Jackson Tennessee. He said, he had gone to church, on time of course, but he sat in the pastor's office with the pastor doing whatever pastors and bishops do. The point is when they came out of the office the service had started, and when they came on to the pulpit other ministers started coming over to them to shake hands and greet them. This action was unpleasing to him because it was bad manners, so he stopped them and said, "This is no time for fellowship. This is worship time; we will have time for fellowship after church." He also said after few minutes into the service ushers came on stage serving juice. So he told them, "We don't need a drink, we just got here and we came right past the water fountain."

Just remember drinking in the pulpit is not good ethics. How does one explain to a five year old child that they don't need water for two hours when adults are drinking/sipping continuously in the pulpit?

PULPIT AIDE

It is important for the pulpit aide to know the rules for serving beverages to people on the pulpit. It is also important to know that you can only follow these rules if those on the pulpit abide by them. *The rule is to serve only those who have exerted themselves in the service, which makes reference to the speakers. But, if anyone seated on the pulpit asks for water, juice, etc, serve them, but only by request.* To refuse anyone would be an insult to the person and an embarrassment to your pastor.

COAT-TAIL PULLING RULE

Years ago pastors would sit directly behind the podium where they preached. So when another minister was allowed to preach, he would be standing directly in front of pastor's seat. If this preacher gets out of order or stayed up too long, the pastor would simply reach out and give his coat tail a couple of tugs. This was a polite way of saying "I'm calling you down, take your seat." After more women became more involved in the teaching and preaching part of church ministry, that rule had to be changed or updated because it would not be polite to pull a woman's coat-tail. Notwithstanding, most pastors didn't allow women in the pulpit or to minister behind the main podium where male preachers stood. Women were directed to use smaller podiums off center stage or down on the floor, However, the Signal was changed so when the speaker got out of order or was too long with their speech, the pastor would interrupt by singing or humming out of sync just loud enough to get the attention of the speaker. The Signal would then be given by eye contact.

Another sign is when the speaker has moved away from the podium and the pastor walks to the main podium, stands directly behind it as though he is the speaker. This is a signal to the speaker, "You are out of order I'll take it from here, you may be seated please."

ASSOCIATE MINISTERS

The question was asked, if the pastor has given an associate minister an opportunity to speak, but on the time the associate is to preach, a visiting minister come in. Should the pastor ask the minister to give up his place that he might share the pulpit with his unexpected guest? My answer to that question is No! The pastor should not have to ask! The associate minister should voluntarily move back and count it an honor to have been asked in the first place.

If you are an associate minister in a local church, and feel your pastor does not allow you to preach in his pulpit as often as he should or you desire; just remember it was not your pastor that called you to preach. It was God, and he didn't call you to preach there! Don't be pushy or impatient, prepare yourself! If God called you, he will use you; when and where is up to Him. I would encourage you to be ready; if he (God) called you, he will send you. The bible says, "Your gift will make room for you." [Proverb 18:16]

**The following topics are in
Question Form.
You judge for yourself.**

CAR WASH

We criticize the business community for using sex to sell merchandise. When we see brochures from auto dealers with a skimpily dressed woman standing by a car that is for sale, we say, "That's terrible, they are using sex to sell cars," I agree. This goes against the principles of this country set by our fore-parents. My question; Is it not just as bad or worse to have our young girls stand on the street holding a sign that says 'CAR WASH' wearing tight shorts and wet T-shirts in the name of the church? This tactic has been proven to work. There is no doubt about it, sex sells cars and sex sells car washes. But, is it good ethics? Is it proper behavior for the church? You judge!

PREACHING BEHIND THE PREACHER

When one preacher or speaker has finished his/her sermon and has taken a seat, would you consider it proper ethics for another preacher, who is not scheduled to preach, to get up and begin preaching the text and continue the same sermon behind him? This is called, preaching behind the preacher. Is this disrespectful to the first preacher? Is it poor ethics, or is it okay? Some preachers are highly offended by this behavior. You be the judge!

FEMALE PASTORS

Some pastors do not accept women as preachers or pastors; Female preachers or pastors are not welcome to sit on the platform or to speak from the pulpit. Whether this is good or bad, right or wrong, I have no comments. However, if members of the female pastor's congregation have been invited to your church to appear on your program and the female pastor comes with her congregation, should she or should she not receive the same respect and honor as any other pastor?

Some pastors will not allow women to sit in their pulpit, even after they have been invited. Do you think it's time to abolish this old tradition? [Women can't sit on the pulpit]. Women have proven to be main liners in the church community and not second class citizens.

PREGNANT SINGLE WOMEN

If a woman who takes an active part in the church ministry becomes pregnant while unmarried, should she be relieved of her duties in the ministry until after the baby is born? Even after she has come before the church and repented? We do know that being pregnant is not the sin, but fornication. Here is the problem. Every time she comes before the church to minister, people will know she is pregnant. People will know she is unmarried. People will know that it's not of the Holy Ghost, as a result when she is up before the congregation in ministry she brings shame to the church. My question: Is this grounds for silencing? In other words should she be asked to sit and not minister in the church until after the baby is born? You judge!

Let's All Practice GOOD Church Ethics!!

COMMENTS
RECEIVED CONCERNING THIS BOOK

What a wonderful vehicle to use along with our church manual in teaching young converts regarding their personal conduct in church. It has generated positive response throughout our state. May God bless Brother Bobby Woods.
-Superintendent / Pastor M. D. Eppright,
Faith Tabernacle COGIC of Des Moines, IA

Every body that goes to church should have one of these little books and put it in action. To me, its worth two million dollars, it has so much good information made simple.
-Mother Flossie Baker of Jackson, TN

This book is very much needed. It didn't come to late... Every church, no matter what denomination, can benefit from it. Brother Woods, thanks for telling us just like it is and reminding us how we should behave in the 'House of God.'
-Mother Bettie Sue Vaughan, State Supervisor of Women
Central Tennessee Jurisdiction C.O.G.I.C.

I highly recommend this little book, it is very beneficial and practical, it will be a great asset to any congregation with the endorsement of the pastor. I commend Brother Bob Woods for his excellent work and his contribution to Christian endeavor.
-Pastor Ozell Northern,
Mt. Ollivet C.O.G.I.C. of Dayton, OH

Church Ethics

COMMENTS
RECEIVED CONCERNING THIS BOOK

I came across this small book titled 'Church Ethics Spelled Out' by Bobby Woods, I have my own personal copy, and I'm using it to teach different sessions at the church where I pastor. I have a Masters of Divinity Degree in Theology, have studied Christian Ethics & Ministerial Ethics. But I believe everyone need this wonderful little book.
-Pastor Melvin Bufford, Mt
Salem M.B. Church, Hickory Valley, TN

This book 'Church Ethics Spelled Out' has truly been a blessing to me and the congregation where I serve as pastor. I like it so much because it's just simple and points out many things that people tends to overlook.
-Pastor William Northern,
Mt. Zion Temple C.O.G.I.C. of Brownsville, TN

This is a very good book, full of good information. It's short and to the point. I feel it will be helpful in restoring reverence and order in our churches during worship services.
-Bishop Jesse E. Williams,
Campbell Chapel M.B. Church of Bolivar, TN

I have read this book of 'Church Ethics'. It is the most detailed book for church rules from the devotion to the benediction. It's a reminder of how we should act in God's house.
-Pastor Junious McTizic,
Zion Temple #2 COGIC of Grand Junction, TN

COMMENTS
RECEIVED CONCERNING THIS BOOK

This book on 'Church Ethics' is much needed in our churches today. People tend to act without thinking and that should not be so in God's house. Brother Woods, I think this book can help us get back to order & respect for the Lord's house. I would that all pastors and church members, especially in Central TN, would get this book, read it and put it in action.
-Bishop W.L. Porter
Prelate Central Tennessee Jurisdiction C.O.G.I.C.

This little book is full of good information. It contains simple guidelines that brings order in God's House. I find when these rules are carried out it makes the pastor's job much easier. Good job Superintendent Woods! I'm pleased to be your pastor.
-Pastor Lazarus Lake,
Zion Temple #1 COGIC of Bolivar TN

I find, 'Church Ethics Spelled Out' a very thought provoking book. It is an excellent reference for those who don't know and a refresher for those who should know. I recommend this book to every pastor, church worker and member. Great Work Uncle Bob!
-Superintendent. James Norman, Bolivar District
St. James COGIC of Grand Junction, TN

Having served as an usher for many years (local, district, state & national), I have witnessed many situations that could have been avoided through the use of this book. I believe this book would serve as an excellent tool to use along with the church member/new member guide upon the approval of the pastor. I commend my vice president on the publishing of this much needed book and I'm Godly proud of his service in Central TN Jurisdiction COGIC Usher board.
-Missionary Dorothy Harris,
President of Central TN Usher Board

COMMENTS
RECEIVED CONCERNING THIS BOOK

This little book, 'Church Ethics Spelled Out' by Bobby woods, was conformation for me. People has to be taught to respect and reverence the house of God. I especially liked the topics concerning: Anointing Oil, Rebuke and Respect to Teachers.
-Pastor Ruby Bledose,
Lighthouse Holiness Church of Bolivar, TN

This book on 'Church Ethics' is much needed for such a time as this. It simply points out areas that shows us that there is always room for improvement. I believe every person that read this book will see the need to change many of their behaviors in God's house.
-Mother Leatha Herron, RN of Valley Stream, NY

I find this book to be a very valuable tool in that it raise ones awareness of how we should behave ourselves in the House of God. It is a house of prayer, a place of worship, not a social club. Thanks, Uncle Bob, for reminding us with such grace and simplicity.
-Prophetess Angela Wimberly, RN of Bloomfield, CT

This book on 'Church Ethics' is so needful in our churches today. I believe every church member should have one of these books. Let us restore Reverence & Honor to God's House.
-Evangelist Theresa Blalark of Jackson, TN

This is an excellent book. I was inspired by it's contents to preach using the subject; "Order in God's House". This writing sets limits & boundaries that men ought to be mindful of in God's house. As Sunday School Superintendent, I find it very helpful.
-Reverend Elizabeth Taylor of Chicago IL

Church Ethics

To contact the author write:

Bobby Woods
756 McTizic Street
Bolivar, TN 38008
or call
Ph: 731-658-9364 or 731-658-0017
Email: bobbyjeanwoods@bellsouth.net

*Please include your testimony of help received from this book
when you write. Your prayer requests are welcomed.*

This book makes
A Perfect Gift
for that friend or relative who has everything
or those really hard to please:

Birthdays, Mother's Day, Father's Day, Christmas
or just to say, *"Thinking of You".*

*It is certainly ideal for your Christian
Brothers & Sisters!*

Bobby L. Woods

www.ingramcontent.com/pod-product-compliance
Lightning Source LLC
Chambersburg PA
CBHW021159080526
44588CB00008B/412